To An
AMAZING TEACHER